HISTORY IN ART

ISLAMIC EMPIRES

Raintree

NICOLA BARBER

www.raintreepublishers.co.uk

Visit our website to find out more information about **Raintree** books.

To order:
☎ Phone 44 (0) 1865 888113
🗎 Send a fax to 44 (0) 1865 314091
💻 Visit the Raintree Bookshop at **www.raintreepublishers.co.uk** to browse our catalogue and order online.

Produced for Raintree by
White-Thomson Publishing Ltd
Bridgewater Business Centre, 210 High Street,
Lewes, East Sussex, BN7 2NH.

First published in Great Britain by Raintree,
Halley Court, Jordan Hill, Oxford OX2 8EJ,
part of Harcourt Education.
Raintree is a registered trademark of Harcourt Education Ltd.

© Harcourt Education Ltd 2005
The moral right of the proprietor has been asserted.

Editorial: Cath Senker and Diyan Leake
Consultant: Dr Tim Insoll, University of Manchester
Design: Michelle Lisseter and Richard Parker
Page make-up: Mind's Eye Design Ltd, Lewes
Illustrations: Encompass Graphics
Picture Research: Elaine Fuoco-Lang
Map artwork: Encompass Graphics
Production: Kevin Blackman
Originated by Ambassador Litho Ltd
Printed and bound in Hong Kong, China
by South China Printing Company

ISBN 1 844 43362 5
09 08 07 06 05
10 9 8 7 6 5 4 3 2 1

British Library Cataloguing in Publication Data
Barber, Nicola
History in Art: Islamic Empires
709.1'767'0902

A full catalogue record for this book is available from the British Library.

Acknowledgements

The publishers would like to thank the following for permission to reproduce photographs (t = top, b = bottom): Art Archive pp. **11, 13, 22** (British Library), **27** (Topkapi Museum Istanbul/Dagli Orti), **31** (t) (Dagli Orti), **37** (b), **39** (b), **43** (t) (Dagli Orti); Bonhams, London pp. **40, 42**; Bridgeman Art Library pp. **5** (t), **5** (b) (Lauros/Giraudon), **6** (t), **6** (b), **7, 9** (both), **10** (t) (Ashmolean Museum), **12, 14** (b) (Index), **14** (t) (Ken Welsh), **15** (Peter Willi), **16** (Giraudon), **18, 19, 20** (t) (Giraudon), **20** (b), **21, 25, 26** (Giraudon), **30, 31** (b), **32, 33** (t), **33** (b) (Giraudon), **34, 35** (both), **36, 39** (t), **41, 45**; British Library p. **24**; British Museum p. **10** (b); The Trustees of the Chester Beatty Library, Dublin p. **43** (b); Corbis pp. **17, 23** (t), **29, 38**; Freer Gallery of Art, Smithsonian Institute p. **28**; Harcourt pp. **1, 3, 8, 23** (b), **37** (t), **44**. Map on p. 4 is by Encompass Graphics.

Cover photograph of an astrolabe reproduced with permission of the Bridgeman Art Library

Every effort has been made to contact copyright holders of any material reproduced in this book. Any omissions will be rectified in subsequent printings if notice is given to the publishers.

The publishers would like to thank Venetia Porter, British Museum, for her assistance in the preparation of this book.

Disclaimer

All the Internet addresses (URLs) given in this book were valid at the time of going to press. However, due to the dynamic nature of the Internet, some addresses may have changed, or sites may have changed or ceased to exist since publication. While the author and publishers regret any inconvenience this may cause readers, no responsibility for any such changes can be accepted by either the author or the publishers.

The paper used to print this book comes from sustainable resources.

Note: When Muslims say the name of one of the prophets, they always say, 'Peace Be Upon Him' afterwards, which is shown in this book as ﷺ.

Contents

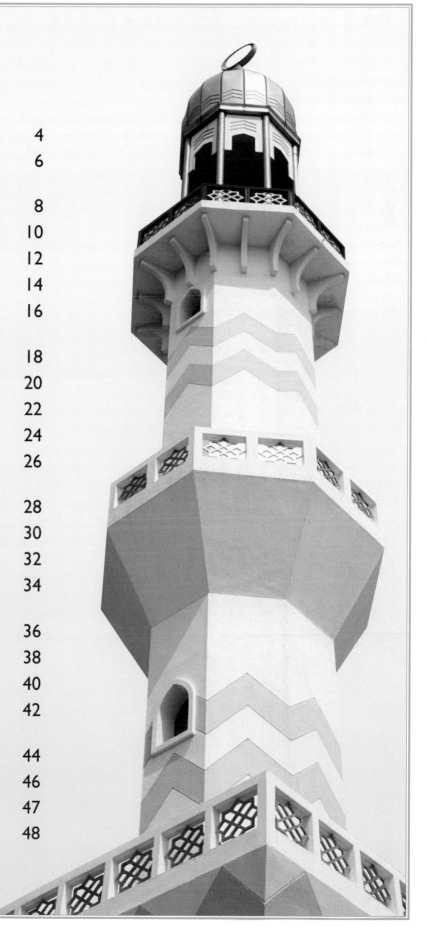

Words included in the glossary are in **bold** the first time
they appear in each chapter.

Art as evidence

This book looks at art over a period of a thousand years – from roughly the seventh to the seventeenth centuries CE – and over an area that stretched from Spain in the west to India in the east. These were the heartlands of an Islamic empire that reached from north-western Africa to South-east Asia. The common feature that linked the peoples of this vast region across this span of time was the religion of Islam. With such a wide geographic spread and long history, Islamic art was inevitably shaped by different regional styles and developments through time. Yet the art of Islam, rooted in the Islamic faith, retained its own unique characteristics throughout the centuries.

▼ This map shows shows the extent of the Islamic Empire on three dates during its long history. The location of the main places mentioned in the text throughout the book are also shown.

The Ka'bah

The Ka'bah (from the Arabic for 'cube') is a simple, cube-shaped structure, built of stone blocks. It contains the black stone, a meteorite that is believed to have been sent from Heaven to Earth. According to Muslim belief, the Ka'bah was built by Ibrahim and his son Ismail, and pilgrimage to the Ka'bah was well established before the time of Muhammad ﷺ. After the Prophet Muhammad ﷺ cleansed the Ka'bah of idols, it became the sacred shrine of Islam. It has remained the *qiblah* (direction of prayer) for Muslims throughout the centuries.

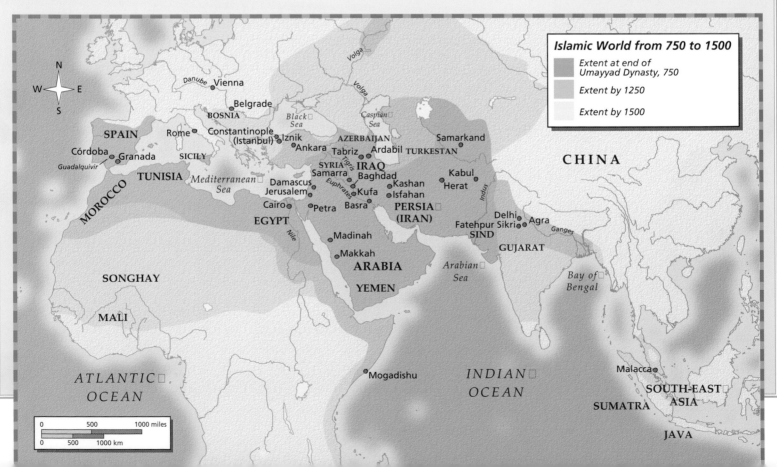

Islamic World from 750 to 1500

- Extent at end of Umayyad Dynasty, 750
- Extent by 1250
- Extent by 1500

Islam arose in the seventh century CE, in Makkah (in present-day Saudi Arabia). A merchant called Muhammadﷺ received a series of revelations, or messages, from Allah. The messages said that he was the one God. At the time, most people in Arabia worshipped many gods and idols. Muhammadﷺ preached this message and converted people to Islam, which means 'submission to the will of Allah'.

The flight to Madinah

Many people in Makkah were unhappy about Islam. In 622 the Prophet Muhammadﷺ and his followers, known as Muslims, left Makkah for Yathrib, a city about 400 kilometres (250 miles) to the north. This city was Muhammad's home for the rest of his life, and was renamed Madinah – 'City of the Prophet'. Muhammadﷺ died in 632, having conquered Makkah and destroyed the idols at the shrine called the Ka'bah.

The birth of Islamic art

The new religion spread quickly across Arabia during Muhammad's lifetime. It continued to spread after his death as his followers conquered neighbouring lands. The Muslims defeated the armies of the **Byzantine** and the **Sasanian** (Persian) empire. They took control of their lands, which today include modern-day Syria, Iraq, Iran, Azerbaijan and Afghanistan. It was this expansion that drew together the ingredients for the birth of Islamic art. The Byzantines and the Persians had highly developed traditions of art and architecture. It was these influences, coupled with the beliefs of the new Islamic faith, that led to the development of a distinctive Islamic art.

▶ The *mihrab* in the mosque of Sheikh Lutfallah in Isfahan, Iran shows some of the distinctive characteristics of Islamic art.

The mihrab *indicates the direction of prayer, the qiblah, for worshippers in the mosque*

This three-dimensional Islamic decoration is known as muqarnas

Calligraphy *is used as surface ornamentation around the* mihrab

Glazed tiles decorate every surface of the interior of the mosque

The development of Islamic art

As the Islamic world expanded, Islamic art and architecture flourished. Styles of architecture developed for important buildings such as mosques, *madrasahs* (Islamic colleges) and palaces. Other arts included metalwork, painting, ceramic pottery and tiles, textiles and carpet-weaving. Looking at objects and asking who made them, who they were made for, and why they were made, gives us a glimpse of life in the Islamic empires.

▶ This ceramic bowl from eastern Iran, is dated from the ninth to tenth century.

The Islamic faith spread rapidly during the seventh and eighth centuries. By 750, the Islamic world stretched from Spain in the west to Afghanistan in the east. In the following centuries, local rulers established dynasties and empires in various parts of the Islamic world. By looking at buildings and artefacts from these empires, we can see that many features of Islamic art were used throughout the Islamic world. Yet each empire also had its own distinctive style, depending on where it was, when it was at the height of its power, and the culture of its people.

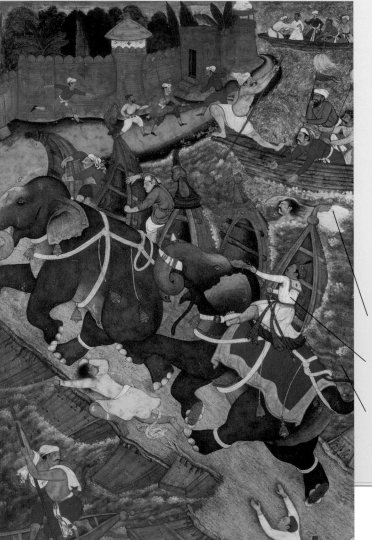

◀ This painting comes from the *Akbarnama (The History of Akbar)*, and dates from the 1590s. The book was commissioned by the **Mughal** emperor Akbar (ruled 1556–1605) and is the story of his life. Illustrations such as these give huge amounts of detailed information about the lives of the Mughal emperors. In the background we see the Red Fort, which was built by Akbar when he moved his capital from Delhi to Agra in 1557.

This is the River Yamuna

Akbar himself is shown taming the savage elephant, Hawa'i

The Akbarnama was written by Akbar's close friend, Abu Fazl, and was illustrated by painters in the royal studios

Many Islamic rulers were enthusiastic and knowledgeable patrons of the arts and sciences. They encouraged scholars from all over the Islamic world to come to their courts and set up workshops for the production of carpets, pottery or metalwork. Some of the artists and craftworkers became famous for their work, for example, the Baghdad calligrapher Ibn al-Bawwab and the **Ottoman** architect Sinan.

Examining the evidence

The history of Islamic coins provides an interesting glimpse of life in early Islamic times. When the Muslims first conquered the Byzantine and Sasanian empires, they continued to use the local currencies. These coins were stamped with the busts of Byzantine or Sasanian emperors and used the Greek and Persian languages. Gradually, the new Arab rulers started to change the coins in a piecemeal way.

It was the **Umayyad** *Khalifah* Abd al-Malik who decided to overhaul the whole system. In 696, he introduced a new Islamic coinage. In line with Islamic tradition (see page 9), the coins contained no images. Instead, the coins showed the *Shahadah*, the Muslim profession of belief in God, and a date. Islamic coins also often carried the name of the place where they were made, and the ruler under whom they were minted. In daily life, these coins reminded everyone of the power of Islam, and of their Muslim rulers.

How has Islamic architecture survived?

The earliest Islamic building to have survived in its original form is the Dome of the Rock in Jerusalem (see page 8), although it has been restored over the centuries. From Spain to India, many other buildings still stand as evidence of the Islamic empires that once held sway. However, some buildings have long been demolished or have disappeared under newer construction. For example, nothing remains of the spectacular circular city of Baghdad. Founded in 762–3 as the capital of the **Abbasid** Empire, it was destroyed by the **Mongols** in 1258 (see page 18) and its ruins lie beneath the modern-day city. For information about these sites, we rely on historical descriptions and, where possible, on archaeology.

▼ The coin from early Umayyad times has verses from the **Qu'ran** stating the oneness of God, the essence of the Islamic faith.

The spread of Islam

After the death of the Prophet Muhammad ﷺ in 632, the leadership of the Islamic community passed in turn to four successors, or *Khalifahs*, known by many Muslims as the *Rashidun* – the 'judicious ones'. The last was Ali ﷺ, cousin of the Prophet Muhammad ﷺ and therefore the only *Khalifah* to be directly related to him. His appointment was the start of a long-lasting division within the Islamic world.

Most Muslims believed that the *Khalifah* should be the person best able to uphold the customs and traditions (the *sunnah*) of Islam; they became known as **Sunni**. Others believed that only someone from the same family as Muhammad ﷺ should become *Khalifah*; they became known as **Shi'a**. In 661, Ali ﷺ was murdered and the governor of Syria, Mu'awiya, seized power. This was the start of the **Umayyad** dynasty, as on Mu'awiya's death the title of *Khalifah* passed to his son. The Umayyads expanded the Islamic Empire both westwards and eastwards.

▼ The Dome of the Rock in Jerusalem. Inside, the sacred rock is enclosed by a circle of pillars that support the dome of the mosque.

The Dome of the Rock

The oldest surviving Muslim building, the Dome of the Rock in Jerusalem, is also one of the most sacred sites in the Islamic world. Arab armies had captured Jerusalem in 638. Work on the mosque began under the Umayyad *Khalifah*, Abd al-Malik, in 685 and was completed in 691. It was built over the rock on Mount Zion from where Muslims believe Muhammad ﷺ went up to Allah on the '**Night of Ascent**'. The construction of the Dome of the Rock sent a powerful message to members of the Jewish and Christian faiths, for whom Jerusalem is also a holy city. The mosque was built on the site of the old Jewish Temple. Inscriptions from the **Qur'an** that adorn the walls take issue with some aspects of Christian belief.

The upper half of the walls is covered with tiles that date from the time of the Ottoman sultan, Sulaiman (see page 26)

The outer shape of the building is an octagon

A panel decorated with words from the Qur'an runs round the building

The lower half of the walls is covered with marble

The Great Mosque

The Great Mosque of Damascus was started by the Umayyad *Khalifah* al-Walid in 705, and completed ten years later. It was a hugely expensive project, designed to create a prestigious place of worship in the Umayyad capital. The mosque was built on the site of a Roman temple, which in turn had been converted into a Christian church by the **Byzantines**. It is a large rectangular building with a courtyard to one side, and it provided a model for the construction of other mosques in the early Islamic world.

◄ Beautiful mosaics decorate some of the outside walls of the Great Mosque of Damascus. This mosaic is on the end of the prayer hall.

The mosaics depict trees and buildings, but there are no human figures

The style of the mosaics points to the influence of Byzantine and Christian art

The mosaics may represent images of Paradise, or may celebrate Umayyad conquests

Idols and images

One striking aspect of the mosaics that decorate both the Dome of the Rock and the Great Mosque of Damascus is that no living beings are represented. There is no specific wording in the Qur'an that forbids the practice. However, it became the tradition very early in Islamic history to avoid the depiction of living things in mosques and other religious buildings, such as *madrasahs* and tombs. It was thought that the representation of figures might lead to the worship of idols (the practice before the time of Muhammadﷺ). It was also believed that the creation of living forms was unique to God. Nevertheless, pictures of people and animals appeared in secular (non-religious) settings such as palaces, and on books, pottery and metalwork.

A detail from the mosaics that decorate the Great Mosque of Damascus

This mosaic used plant-like patterns

Mosaic is made from small pieces of glass

The Abbasids

The **Abbasids** came to power in 750, having seized control from the Umayyads. They moved the capital of the Islamic Empire from Damascus to Iraq, establishing a new capital city in Baghdad in 762–3. The peak of the Abbasid Empire came during the reign of *Khalifah* Harun al-Rashid (786–809), who ruled over a court of great ceremony and opulence. His court was the setting for the tales that make up the *Thousand and One Nights*, although they were not collected and written down until much later.

▶ This lustreware bowl dates from the ninth century and was made in Samarra, in Iraq. It has a shiny **lustre** glaze. Such pottery was made to satisfy the demands from the Abbasid court for luxury ware.

▼ This fragment is from a reconstruction of a wall painting from the Jawsaq al-Khaqani palace in Samarra. The palace was the residence of the Khalifah during the time that the Abbasids inhabited Samarra as their capital.

The figure faces forward in a pose typical of Sasanian styles

The painting comes from the harem – the women's quarters in the palace

Looking east

During the excavation of an Abbasid palace in Samarra, which began in 1911, fragments of a wall-painting were discovered. It shows two women dancers pouring wine, and it decorated a wall in the **harem** (women's quarters) of the palace. The style shows the influence of **Sasanian** art from the Persian Empire conquered by the Muslims in the seventh century. It underlines the increasing importance of Persian influences in the Islamic Empire, after the Abbasids moved the capital eastwards. As a result of this move, the Abbasids distanced themselves from Arabia and the traditional heartland of Islam. They relied on Persian bureaucrats to run the empire, and Persian troops to defend them. Like the earlier Sasanian rulers, the Abbasid *Khalifahs* lived in opulent imperial style, very different from the simple, religious lives of the Prophet Muhammad ﷺ and the *Rashidun*.

Samarra

In about 836, unrest in Baghdad between the local population and Turkish troops in the Abbasid army drove the Abbasids to abandon their capital and move 90 kilometres (60 miles) north to Samarra. The Abbasids stayed in Samarra for just over 50 years, returning to Baghdad in 892. A new city quickly developed at Samarra, stretching some 30 kilometres (20 miles) along the River Tigris. Under *Khalifah* al-Mutawakkil (ruled 847–61),

huge building works were undertaken, including the Great Mosque and many lavish palaces. Building work stopped when the Abbasids returned to Baghdad, and much of the population left the city. For archaeologists, Samarra has been a rich source of information about Islamic art. It was inhabited for a very short period, allowing them to accurately date styles of pottery and carving.

▶ The Great Mosque in Samarra was built between 849 and 851 and was the biggest in the Islamic world. Outside the main courtyard stood a conical **minaret** with a spiral ramp winding round its outside.

The shape of the minaret was probably influenced by the ziggurats of the ancient Assyrians

Spiral ramp

The minaret is 53 metres high

The minaret sits on a square base

The minaret is built of brick

The round city

The second Abbasid *Khalifah*, al-Mansur (ruled 754–75), built Baghdad at the meeting point of several important trade routes. The city quickly became a commercial hub. Nothing remains of the original city of Baghdad – much was destroyed by the **Mongols** in 1258 and the remainder has been built over.

We know from descriptions that Baghdad was a circular city, with the *Khalifah's* imposing royal palace and a large mosque in the middle. The symbolic message of this design was clear. The *Khalifah* was at the centre of the Islamic world and far removed from ordinary Muslims.

Architecture

The most basic and most typical type of architecture found throughout the Islamic world was a house with a courtyard. Such houses were suited to the hot climates of most Islamic countries. They also reflected the culture of Islamic societies, in which women were shielded from the outside world, and the privacy of the family was highly valued. This emphasis on the inside space, rather than the outside, is seen in architecture throughout the Islamic world. There are certain architectural features that are found all over the Islamic world. Some, such as the minaret, the **mihrab** and the **minbar** are particular features of a mosque.

Main features

Other features, such as domes, courtyards and arches, are found in all types of building. In Central Asia and Persia, a typical feature was the **iwan**, an open-air hall with an arched ceiling. This came originally from the Sasanians and was used in mosques, *madrasahs* (Islamic colleges), **caravanserais** and tombs.

▼ This is the courtyard of the Friday Mosque in Isfahan, looking towards the *iwan*. There are four *iwans* in the huge courtyard, one on each side. This layout became common in mosques and *madrasahs* in central Asia.

The roof of the iwan *is decorated with ornamental vaults called* muqarnas

The mosque dates from the twelfth century, but the minarets were added in the seventeenth century

The qiblah iwan – *it shows the direction of prayer towards Makkah*

The surface of the building is decorated with glazed tiles

In their buildings, Islamic architects aimed to create a sense of weightlessness and light. This was achieved partly by the use of extensive decoration on every surface. Mosaics reflected light, and carved stonework cut away the heaviness of supporting walls. These helped to create the feeling of airiness that is the hallmark of some of the greatest Islamic architectural triumphs.

Types of building

A mosque was a basic requirement for any Muslim community. Mosques, ranging from small local mosques to the large communal Friday mosques used for the main service of the week, were built everywhere in the Islamic world.

The construction of tombs in the Islamic world was more controversial, because the glorification of the dead was not part of Islamic tradition. Nevertheless, from the time of the **Seljuks** (990–1118), wealthy rulers constructed **mausoleums** in preparation for their deaths. Many Islamic rulers built large complexes, which often included a mosque and a *madrasah*. *Madrasahs* were places of learning where students studied the Islamic religion and Islamic law. Many Sunni *madrasahs* were founded by the Seljuks, partly in reaction to the threat from the Shi'a **Fatimids** in Egypt (see page 16).

◀ This is the funerary complex of the Mamluk sultan Qa'itbay (reigned 1468–96). It contained a *madrasah*, a mosque, the tomb of Qa'itbay, a hospice and a source of clean water.

Al-Andalus

When the Abbasids took power, the first action of the new *Khalifah* was to massacre members of the Umayyad clan in order to secure his authority over the Islamic Empire. But an Umayyad prince called Abd al-Rahman escaped. He made his way across North Africa to Spain, where he defeated the Abbasid ruler in 756. He established an independent Islamic state, called al-Andalus, in southern Spain. By the tenth century it had become a renowned centre for learning and the arts.

▲ This magnificent dome was added to the Great Mosque of Córdoba in the tenth century. A glittering mosaic decorates the interior of the dome. It is made from gold cubes that were brought from the Byzantine Empire.

The Great Mosque at Córdoba

Abd al-Rahman founded a dynasty that was to rule over al-Andalus for nine generations. He made his capital at Córdoba, on the north bank of the River Guadalquivir. There he began to construct a mosque that would be large enough for all of the city's Muslim citizens to meet for prayer. He also started other construction projects including palaces, mosques, bath houses, gardens and fountains. Córdoba became one of the most celebrated cities in the Islamic world.

◀ This is the interior of the Great Mosque in Córdoba. The double arches were inspired by the arches of the Great Mosque in Damascus, and possibly also by Roman aqueducts in Spain.

The double arches were used to raise the height of the roof

The upper arches are supported by short piers

The red colour in the arches is brick, the white is stone – the contrast is made greater with paint

The lower arches rest on columns

By constructing the Great Mosque, Abd al-Rahman and his successors tried to recreate the splendours lost to the Umayyads in Syria. The mosque was built from 784 to 786, but it was enlarged three times over subsequent centuries. Craftworkers came from afar to work on the mosque – not from the main Islamic Empire, which was under the control of the Abbasid enemy, but from Christian Constantinople, which remained under the rule of the Byzantines. The Umayyads maintained good relations with the Byzantines, as they largely did with the Christian and Jewish populations in al-Andalus. These groups were tolerated as long as they did not rebel against their Muslim rulers.

Palace splendours

The Umayyad dynasty reached its peak in al-Andalus under the rule of Abd al-Rahman III (912–61), who proclaimed himself *Khalifah* in 929. He founded a new capital just outside Córdoba called Madinat al-Zahra. It had a palace, government offices and housing for up to 20,000 staff. Only ruins survive of Madinat al-Zahra, but the splendour of life at the Spanish Umayyad court can be glimpsed through the exquisite carved ivory caskets that were a favourite of wealthy courtiers. The ivory was from Africa, and came from elephant and hippopotamus tusks. The caskets were used to store jewellery or perfumes. Their decoration often included figures and animals as well as inscriptions stating the name of the owner.

The Alhambra

The rule of the Umayyads in Spain was replaced in the eleventh century by the **Berber Almoravid** and **Almohad** dynasties. At the same time, the Christian reconquest of Spain began. By the end of the thirteenth century, the only remaining Muslim stronghold was Granada. The rulers of Granada, the Nasrids, lived in a fortified palace called the Alhambra, built between 1238 and 1358. Today, it is one of the best preserved palaces of the Islamic world. Like the Topkapi Sarai in Istanbul (see page 26), its layout reflects the Islamic preference for a maze-like collection of courts and rooms rather than a grand, balanced design such as is seen in many European palaces. The Alhambra contains some exquisite stone carving as well as beautiful gardens.

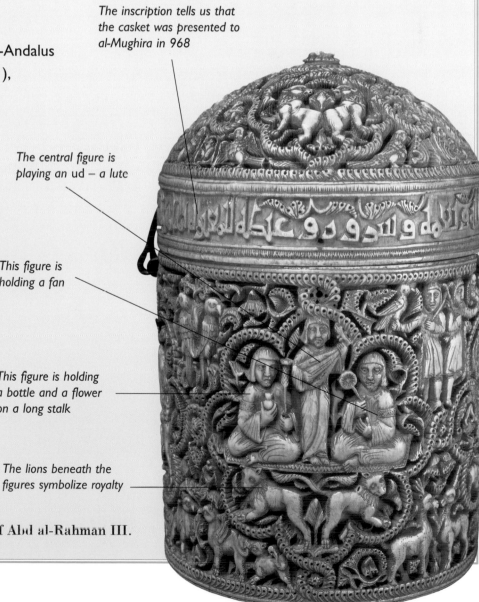

The inscription tells us that the casket was presented to al-Mughira in 968

The central figure is playing an ud – a lute

This figure is holding a fan

This figure is holding a bottle and a flower on a long stalk

The lions beneath the figures symbolize royalty

▶ This casket was made for al-Mughira, son of Abd al-Rahman III.

The Fatimids

By the tenth century, the Abbasid *Khalifah* had been reduced to little more than a figurehead, as rival groups seized power in various parts of the Islamic world. The Seljuk Turks, who converted to Islam in the 990s, seized power from the Abbasids in the eleventh century. In 969, the Fatimids defeated the Abbasid rulers in Egypt, and in 973 established their capital at al-Qahirah, 'the triumphant' – known as Cairo in English. Unlike the Abbasids and Seljuks, who were Sunni Muslims, the Fatimids were Shi'as, and their leader claimed descent from Fatimah, daughter of the Prophet Muhammadﷺ.

Wealth and prosperity

The Fatimid Empire was very prosperous because of the wealth from Egyptian agriculture and Egypt's position at the centre of the profitable trade between the Mediterranean and lands to the east. This prosperity was reflected in the opulence of the Fatimid court. The Fatimid rulers surrounded themselves with beautiful pottery, glass, metalwork, and other objects such as this ewer made from rock crystal. Many of these objects were made in the workshops of al-Fustat, old Cairo. Fatimid craftworkers became renowned for their creativity and skills. Cairo soon rivalled Baghdad as a cultural and artistic centre.

▶ This ewer, made from rock crystal, dates from the tenth century. Rock crystal was imported to Egypt from Arabia, Iraq and East Africa. It was used to make glasses, ewers and basins for holding liquids. The purity of rock crystal also reminded Muslims of words in the Qur'an that refer to the crystal cups from which true believers drink in Paradise.

Rock crystal was highly prized because it was supposed to shatter if it came into contact with poison – the person using it could trust that the drink was safe

The crystal was hollowed out to make ewers and other vessels, and then carved on the outside

Shi'a Islam

When the Fatimids founded Cairo, they built a large mosque called al-Azhar – 'the splendid'. This mosque became a centre of learning, and is still a university today. During the Fatimid period it was the focus for the teaching of Shi'a Islam. While the Fatimids waged war on the Sunni Abbasids, they also attempted to convert Abbasid subjects to Shi'a Islam. They did this through the use of *da'is* – missionaries. Al-Azhar became a training centre for *da'is*. However, despite this programme of conversion, Sunni Islam remained widespread. Then in 1169 Salah ad-Din seized power and two years later proclaimed a return to Sunni Islam in Egypt.

The Fatimid Treasury

What evidence do we have today of life at the Fatimid court? In fact, very little, since the Fatimid palaces have disappeared. Many of the sumptuous objects made during the period have been destroyed. During the eleventh century there was famine and political unrest in Egypt. Between 1067 and 1072 the Great Treasury, where the Fatimids stored their most precious objects, was repeatedly looted. Many objects were smashed, sold or melted down. Luckily, two detailed descriptions of the Great Treasury survive, giving us a glimpse of the huge and priceless collection of the *Khalifah*. One description lists 36,000 items of rock crystal.

▼ The view looking down into the courtyard of the al-Azhar mosque in Cairo, Egypt.

The mosque has two minarets

The dome was built in the twelfth century

The mosque was founded in 970; the façade of the courtyard was added later

17

The great empires

The **Mongols** were **nomads** who came from the steppes of Central Asia. In 1206, they formed a confederation of tribes under a leader called Genghis Khan (ruled 1206–27). The Mongols first attacked China, before turning their attentions to the Islamic lands to the west. In 1258, Genghis's grandson Hulagu sacked Baghdad, finally bringing the rule of the *Abbasid Khalifahs* to an end. It was the first time that the Islamic world had been overwhelmed by non-Muslims. The Mongols wreaked havoc as they conquered, leaving a trail of death and destruction behind them.

Conversion and reconstruction

In the years following the sack of Baghdad, the Mongol khan (emperor) converted to Islam. By the beginning of the fourteenth century, many Mongols had followed his example and adopted Islam. The Mongols began a process of reconstruction, rebuilding the cities they had destroyed in even more splendid architectural styles than before. They also became great patrons of the arts and sciences, encouraging poetry, painting, and the study of astronomy and history.

▶ This illustration is taken from a book by Rashid al-Din. It shows the Mongol leader Genghis Khan in battle.

The *Jami al-Tawarikh* (*World History*) of Rashid al-Din was produced in Tabriz, Iran, in the early fourteenth century. Rashid al-Din was vizier (chief minister) to the Mongol khan Ghazan. He was also a historian. His book included not only an account of the Prophet Muhammad ﷺ and his followers, but also of the Jews, the Chinese, the Indians, and the Turkish and Mongol tribes. Several copies were made and illustrated, in both the Arabic and Persian languages. The Mongol patronage of such work showed their desire to mark their own place in history and in the Islamic world.

Samarkand splendour

By the middle of the fourteenth century, Mongol power was fading. Timur, the last Mongol conqueror, attempted to reverse this decline. From the 1380s until his death in 1405, Timur established control over much of Central Asia, Iran and Iraq, capturing Delhi, India in the east and

Timur the Lame (*c.*1336–1405)

Timur (known as 'the Lame') was born near Samarkand and claimed descent from Genghis Khan. He was determined to bring the Islamic world under Mongol rule and set about this task with great ruthlessness. It is said that in 1387, after his defeat of Isfahan, a tower of 70,000 human skulls was erected to deter any would-be opponents. In 1398 he invaded India, sacking Delhi and massacring its inhabitants. Nevertheless, Timur was a devout Muslim and a great patron of arts and architecture. During his lifetime and after his death, he captured the imagination of Muslim and non-Muslim alike. In the sixteenth century, the English playwright Christopher Marlowe wrote a play about him, *Tamberlaine the Great*.

Ankara (in modern-day Turkey) in the west. He made his capital at Samarkand, and took back wealth, scholars and craftworkers from all over his newly conquered empire. The results of Timur's patronage of art and architecture can be seen today in buildings such as the Gur-i Amir.

▼ Timur himself was buried in the Gur-i Amir, although the tomb was originally built for one of his grandsons. The inside of the Gur i Amir tomb uses materials of great richness for decoration, including alabaster, onyx, marble, jasper and gold.

The shape of the bulbous dome that crowns the building is typical of Timurid architecture

The ribbed dome is covered with tiles

The huge calligraphy on the drum reads, 'Allah is eternal'

The Safavids

The **Safavids** came originally from Azerbaijan, near the Caspian Sea; they took their name from their founder, Safi al-Din. They established their rule in 1501, when they captured Tabriz, and quickly extended their empire across Iran and into Iraq. The Safavids were **Shi'a** Muslims. Throughout their rule they battled against their **Sunni** Muslim neighbours for territory – the **Ottomans** to the west and the **Uzbeks** to the northeast.

▲ This painting of Shah Abbas I dates from the seventeenth century and comes from Mughal India.

The Ardabil carpet

The most famous and successful of the Safavid rulers was Shah Abbas I (reigned 1588–1629), also known as Abbas the Great. He established the Safavid capital at Isfahan, and encouraged the production of superb textiles, carpets and pottery. Shah Abbas intended that such industries would provide the basis for the prosperity of the Safavid Empire. Isfahan soon became a commercial centre, with merchants from all parts of the world visiting the city. There was already a long tradition of carpet weaving in the region, but Shah Abbas established large workshops for the production of high-quality carpets. The carpets varied in size from small prayer rugs to huge carpets, and many were intended for export.

▼ This carpet dates from 1539–40. It is known as the Ardabil carpet, because it was probably made for the Safavid shrine in Ardabil.

The inscription on the carpet reads: 'Except for thy heaven, there is no refuge for me in this world. Other than here there is no place for my head. Work of a servant of the court, Maqsud of Kashan, 946'

The carpet is made from wool and silk, and measures 10.9 x 5.3 metres

Mosque lamps hang from the central star of the pattern

The carpet has between 46 and 50 knots per square centimetre, making possible the fine detail of the pattern

Isfahan

The reconstruction of Isfahan as the new capital of the Safavid Empire (the previous capital was at Tabriz) started in 1597. The city was a tribute to the commercial and military policies of Shah Abbas. Under his rule, the economy of the empire was flourishing and its borders were secure from the Uzbeks and Ottomans. At the time, Isfahan was one of the largest cities in the world, with a population of about one million people. The majestic buildings in the city impressed visitors, as did the streets lined with plane trees, the canals and parks, and the huge **bazaar** – a centre for trade that covered 30 square kilometres (12 square miles). At the centre of the city was the Maydan-i Shah, a large public square that formed the heart of the city. It provided space for markets, polo games and ceremonial occasions.

Riza-i Abbasi (d.1635)

Painting flourished at the Abbasid court, and the leading painter of the early seventeenth century was Riza-i Abbasi. His paintings were either book illustrations, or were collected into loose-leaf albums. The Safavids were great lovers of books, a reminder of their origins as nomads, people who prized portable possessions. Riza-i Abbasi developed a new style of painting that was far more naturalistic (lifelike) than anything seen before. He not only painted refined courtly figures but also ordinary people such as soldiers, peasants and musicians.

▼ This picture shows the southern end of the great public space in Isfahan, called the Maydan-i Shah.

This is the entrance to the Shah Mosque

This is the Maydan-i Shah

This is the courtyard of the Shah Mosque

This is the qiblah iwan

The Maydan-i Shah was lined with shops

The Mughals

The word '**Mughal**' is a form of 'Mongol'. The first Mughal ruler, Babur (emperor 1526–30), traced his descent back to both Genghis Khan and Timur. Babur invaded India in the early 1500s, establishing an empire that at its height in the sixteenth and seventeenth centuries covered the whole country except for the southernmost tip. We know a great deal about the lives of Babur and the other great Mughal emperors from detailed miniature paintings. The Mughals were also responsible for some spectacular buildings, including Akbar's city, Fatehpur Sikri, and the Taj Mahal, built by Shah Jahan.

A vision of paradise

Babur was a brilliant leader and general. He spent much of his life on the battlefield, but he nevertheless found time to write poetry and his memoirs, called the *Babur-nama*. These memoirs were later illustrated by painters who worked in studios at the Mughal court. Paintings in the *Babur-nama* reveal Babur's love of gardens. He created beautiful, formal gardens, where water ran along straight channels and played gently in fountains. The sound and sight of running water was highly prized in Islamic gardens, partly because of the hot, dry climate of much of the Islamic world. Fountains and rivers are also frequently mentioned in the **Qur'an** as a vision of Paradise. After his death in 1530, Babur was buried in his favourite garden in Kabul, Afghanistan.

▼ This illustration comes from the *Babur-nama* (*The History of Babur*), which was completed in about 1589. Akbar commissioned the illustrations for his grandfather's memoirs. This painting shows nobles being entertained in a beautiful garden.

Babur sits on a carpet beneath a canopy

Musicians are playing drums, a lute and a woodwind instrument

At the centre of the garden is a fountain

A dancer provides entertainment

22

Akbar the Great

Although Babur established the Mughal Empire in India, it was his grandson Akbar (reigned 1556–1605) who extended and secured it. Akbar was fascinated by other religions and adopted a policy of tolerance towards all faiths in his empire. Evidence of Akbar's interests can be seen at Fatehpur Sikri, the new capital city that he built. The style of the buildings at Fatehpur Sikri combined Muslim domes, arches and courts with traditional Hindu designs. At the centre of the city was the *Diwan-i-Khas* – the hall of private audience. In this small pavilion, Akbar would sit and debate with religious scholars. Fatehpur Sikri was abandoned in the 1580s, but the buildings still stand today.

Fatehpur Sikri was built on a ridge overlooking the surrounding countryside

Walkways from the central throne connect it to the screened balcony

Inside the Diwan-i-Khas is a central pillar that supports a raised throne

The whole city was built from red sandstone

▲ This small pavilion is the *Diwan-i-Khas* – the hall of private audience – at Fatehpur Sikri in India. It was built for Akbar in the sixteenth century.

A monument to love

The Taj Mahal was built by the Mughal emperor Shah Jahan (reigned 1627–58) as a tomb for his beloved wife Mumtaz Mahal. She died in 1631, giving birth to their fifteenth child. The Taj Mahal is evidence of the huge wealth of the Mughal emperors, who could afford the finest craftsworkers and materials from all over the Islamic world for their building projects. Craftsworkers from Turkey, Afghanistan, Persia and Central Asia worked on the Taj Mahal, alongside Muslim and Hindu workers from the Mughal Empire itself.

Painting

The art of painting was one of the glories of the Islamic empires. Secular paintings were used to illustrate books (although no images were used to decorate the Qur'an), and were therefore often miniature in size and exquisitely detailed. The first illustrated books date from the twelfth century, but very few examples survive today. Illustrations were used in the translations made from Greek works and other sources, but the first major flowering of the art of painting happened in Persia in the fourteenth century.

Persian painting

During the fourteenth century, the Mongol Empire stretched from the Middle East to the Far East. The links between Persia and China encouraged a new style of painting. The *Shahnama* – a long poem recounting the adventures of the Persian kings – was a favourite for illustration. Another work that became very popular was the *Khamseh* (*Five Poems*) of Nizami. An illustration made in the Safavid court for one of the Khamseh marks an important break in Islamic tradition. It portrays the ascent of Muhammad ﷺ to the heavens on the **Night of Ascent** (see page 8). The figure of the Prophet is represented, although his face is veiled so that his features cannot be seen.

These are verses from Nizami's poem

▶ This illustration comes from a copy of the *Khamseh* (*Five Poems*) of Nizami. The book was illustrated from 1539 to 1543 for the Safavid ruler, Shah Tahmasp.

The illustration shows a musician, Barbad, playing the lute to an Iranian prince, Khusraw

The Ottomans

The Ottoman sultans (see pages 26–7) set up a royal studio of painters in Istanbul, with artists from all parts of the empire. The painters brought with them a wide range of styles and expertise. Accounts of Sultan Sulaiman's campaigns were illustrated with paintings full of realistic detail, as well as bird's-eye-view maps of places such as Lepanto, Genoa and Venice. In the 1550s, Sulaiman ordered the creation of a history of the Ottomans in five volumes. The fifth, the *Suleymannama*, dealt with his own reign, and was completed in 1588. The elegance with which the court painters depicted their subjects marked a new stage in the development of the Ottoman miniature.

The Mughals

The Mughal emperors Akbar, Jahangir and Shah Jahan took a great interest in miniature painting and, as at the Ottoman court in Istanbul, there was a large royal studio. Illustrations were made for histories of the Mughals, as well as portraits of the emperors themselves. Jahangir took a particular interest in nature. There are many exquisite illustrations of animals from the time of his reign, such as zebras, elephants, exotic birds and horses.

▼ This zebra was painted for the Mughal emperor Jahangir by one of his favourite court painters, Mansur, in 1621. The zebra was brought to the Mughal court from Abyssinia (modern-day Ethiopia).

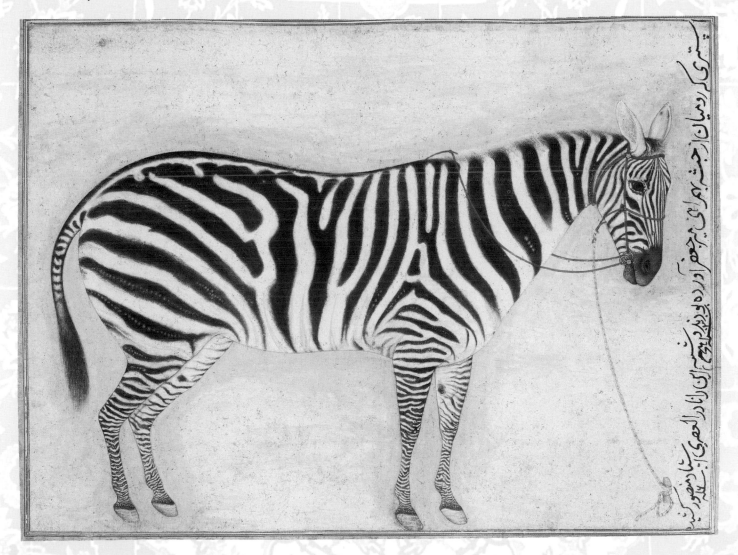

The Ottomans

The Ottomans were descended from nomadic tribes in Anatolia. They established their empire in the region where Europe meets Asia, in modern-day Turkey. In 1453, the Ottomans captured Constantinople from the Byzantines and made it the capital of their empire, renaming it Istanbul. In 1514, the Ottomans defeated the Safavids at Chaldiran, and temporarily captured the Safavid capital, Tabriz. In the west, the greatest of the Ottoman sultans, Sulaiman 'the Magnificent' (reigned 1520–66), extended Ottoman power across Hungary, threatening both Vienna and Rome with his formidable armies.

This painting can be found at the sultan's grand palace in Istanbul, the Topkapi Sarai, which today is a museum. It shows the siege of Belgrade in 1521, with the brightly coloured tents of the Ottoman army on the right, and the besieged city on the left. Sulaiman sits in splendour in his tent while members of the Janissary troops can be seen below, recognizable from their tall hats with a fold of cloth dangling from the back. Some of these highly respected troops were Christian youths. They had been selected to become Muslims, and to receive a strict, thorough education until the age of 25, when they joined the Janissary corps.

◄ This illustration, painted by an artist called Lokman, comes from the *Hunernama*, one of the finest illustrated works containing historical paintings from the Ottoman era. It dates from 1588.

Sulaiman sits in his tent

The Ottomans used cannon to bombard the city

Janissary troops are recognizable by their hats, which were a sign of their obedience to a holy man, Hajji Bektash

The Ottoman court

The Ottomans had an extremely efficient state bureaucracy that ran all aspects of the empire. The sultan stood at the head of the state with absolute authority. Beneath him, the bureaucracy was divided into three areas: the imperial council and treasury, the military, and the Muslim legal system.

There was a strict hierarchy, and it was often possible to assess the rank and even occupation of a person from their dress. The sultans and their courtiers wore magnificent kaftans, often made from silk. On their heads, they wore large turbans, often topped with a jewelled medallion.

Members of the Janissaries wore tall hats, while the sultans' bodyguards wore hats with tall, white plumes. We know about these modes of dress from illustrations, and from the magnificent robes preserved in the Topkapi Sarai in Istanbul.

▶ This kaftan was worn by the Ottoman sultan Bayezid II.

The kaftan is made from silk

The sleeves are short

There are buttons down to the waist

Gold braid, called 'frogging', decorates the front

The style of decoration of many Ottoman silks was similar to that found on ceramics such as tile panels

Sinan (1489–1588)

Sinan was probably from a Greek family, but became a Janissary in 1521 and went on to have a successful military career. He came to the notice of the sultan because of his work as a military engineer. In 1538 he was appointed court architect, a post he held until his death. During this time he worked on over 400 buildings. These included the Topkapi Sarai, the Shehzade Mosque and the Sulaimaniye Mosque, all in Istanbul. Sinan was fascinated by the huge dome of the **Byzantine** cathedral in Istanbul, St Sophia, which was over a thousand years old. Under Muslim rule, St Sophia was converted into a mosque, but Sinan was determined to build a wider dome. He eventually managed it. The dome of the Selimiye Mosque at Edirne, which was completed in 1575, spanned 31 metres.

Life in the Islamic empires

Life for the people of the many empires and dynasties of the Islamic world varied hugely according to the influences of geography, climate and culture. Yet the traditions and laws of Islam meant that as far apart as Africa and India, some aspects of everyday life were remarkably similar. Many of the daily customs that linked people across the Islamic world were to do with observance of the 'Five Pillars' of Islam, the main rules for Muslim life (see pages 38–9). Others were habits and customs that had been passed down for generations.

Nomadic roots

Some Arabs were settled, but many were **nomads** or semi-nomads, who inhabited the arid desert regions of the Arabian peninsula. Agriculture was possible in parts of southern Arabia, and around the oases in central and eastern regions. The remainder of the land, however, was suitable only for grazing camels, sheep and goats. The Arab tribespeople moved from place to place, looking for grazing land for their animals. After the Islamic conquests, many Arabs began to live increasingly settled and urban lives.

Other nomadic peoples included the **Seljuks** and the **Mongols**. The nomadic life meant that possessions that could be easily transported were highly prized. This led to the widespread use and love of carpets throughout the Islamic world, as well as the patronage of fine books by many Islamic rulers.

▼ This illustration is from the *Divan* (*Collected Poems*) of Sultan Ahmad, a ruler of the Jalayirids who held power in Iraq and Azerbaijan in the fourteenth and fifteenth centuries.

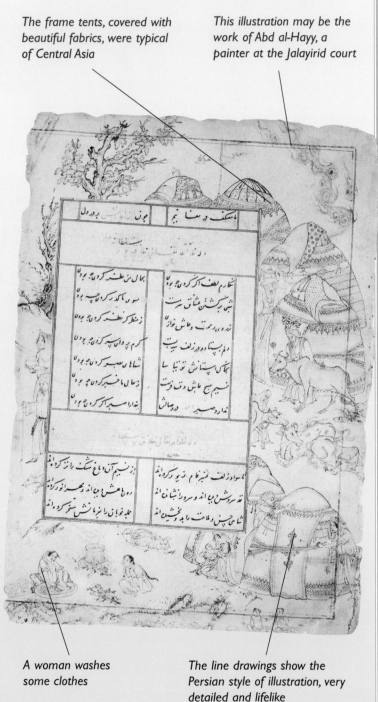

The frame tents, covered with beautiful fabrics, were typical of Central Asia

This illustration may be the work of Abd al-Hayy, a painter at the Jalayirid court

A woman washes some clothes

The line drawings show the Persian style of illustration, very detailed and lifelike

▶ This is an aerial view of the town of Kairouan in Tunisia, north Africa. At the centre of the town lies the Great Mosque of Kairouan, which dates from the tenth century.

This is the Great Mosque of Kairouan

There are no windows on the street side of the houses

Narrow streets run between the houses

Each house has an interior courtyard

This is the central courtyard

This is the minaret

Home life

The tents of the Arab nomads were divided into men's and women's areas, and the same division was found in houses throughout the Islamic world. For Muslims, the house was a place of privacy and security. This was reflected in the architecture of Islamic homes, which had high exterior walls, often without windows. Inside, a house was usually designed around a courtyard, or several courtyards. These areas allowed for outdoor activity with shelter from the wind and sun. A large part of the house was the women's area, or **harem** (related to the Arabic word *haram*, meaning 'sacred'). The *harem* was forbidden to all men except husbands and sons. Male guests to the house were entertained in the men's reception room.

The bazaar

The commercial centre of any Muslim town was the **bazaar**. This bustling market district was often roofed to provide shelter from the fierce sun. The commercial quarter of a town was usually separate from the residential areas, and different trades and goods were often grouped together. For example, the large bazaars in Istanbul, Cairo and Baghdad had separate quarters for leather goods, spices, food, metal, jewellery and textiles, amongst others. The bazaars were well regulated; market inspectors were responsible for checking weights and measures, and the quality of goods.

Ceramics

Ceramic ware (pottery) was used from the earliest times for practical, everyday use – mainly storing, cooking and serving food. Earthenware pots were the most basic type of vessel, but early potters soon discovered how to paint a glaze on to an earthenware pot. A glaze is a thin, glassy layer that makes the pot waterproof.

From **Abbasid** times, the decoration of pottery became increasingly lavish. New techniques of creating surface pattern and colour were constantly being developed and perfected. Coloured ceramic tiles were used to decorate buildings all over the Islamic world, but most notably in Persia and Anatolia (part of modern-day Turkey). The production of all types of ceramics came to a peak in workshops such as those at Isnik during the time of the **Ottoman** Empire.

Lustreware

One of the earliest techniques that was perfected by Islamic potters was the application of **lustre** glazes. The first examples of this technique come from the Abbasid period, but the application of lustre was developed and perfected in many centres in the Islamic world. Lustre glazes contained a metallic **pigment** that gave the colour sparkle once the object had been fired in a kiln. This technique proved popular partly because it allowed the potter to mimic precious metals such as gold and silver.

A man sits with five women

The figures are curved to allow them to fit the shape of the dish

The decoration is painted in a brown lustre

The dish is made from fritware, a white material made from quartz and clay

▲ This bowl was made in 1211–12 in Kashan, a major centre of ceramic production in Persia.

Tilework

Glazed tiles are a characteristic decoration for buildings in the central Islamic world. The patterns and the brilliant colours – often turquoises and blues – create stunning effects on buildings such as the great mosques of Isfahan. There were several different techniques used in tilework. Sometimes pieces of tile were cut to make a mosaic. Alternatively, whole tiles were coloured and decorated to form part of a larger pattern. These tiles were often decorated using the *cuerda seca* (dry cord) technique. The tiles were painted with different colours, which were separated by a greasy black paste. When the tiles were fired in the kiln, the paste formed a black line between the colours.

▶ This tiled panel comes from the Friday Mosque in Isfahan, Iran. Each individual tile forms part of a larger pattern.

Isnik

During the Ottoman period, pottery in the Anatolian region was dominated by production at Isnik. For many centuries, Islamic pottery had been influenced by imports from China. Much of the pottery produced at Isnik was in the Chinese style, with brilliant white backgrounds and mostly blue designs. Isnik was also a centre for tile manufacture and the production of superb large panels of decoration for the palaces and mosques of Istanbul and elsewhere. The motifs that were used for ceramic decoration were also used on the silks and luxurious fabrics that were sewn into costumes for courtiers.

◀ This bowl comes from Isnik in Turkey and dates from the sixteenth century. The clear blue and white colours are typical of one style of pottery made in Isnik.

Entitlement

Poetry and music were very popular forms of entertainment at courts throughout the Islamic world. However, because of the tradition of avoiding the depiction of living beings, theatre did not flourish in most Islamic societies. The same prohibitions also affected traditions of dance. Nevertheless, shadow puppet plays were popular in Egypt, and the Ottomans staged huge pageants with lavish music and theatrical productions to celebrate major events.

Music

In the Islamic world, religious music was confined to the call to prayer (the **adhan**) and the chanting of the **Qur'an**. However, the Arabic word *musiqa* excludes these religious forms, and refers mainly to secular vocal and instrumental music. Such music was used in the Islamic world at all major events, such as weddings, pilgrimages and celebrations. Although little music was ever written down, it has been passed down the generations and much of this traditional music is still played today.

Music was a very important form of court entertainment, and some musicians were highly paid and greatly appreciated by their royal employers. There are many images showing an Islamic ruler with his prized court musician. There are also many images of musicians playing instruments, which give us useful information about the type of music that was being played.

▶ The illustration on the right shows a scene at the court of an Islamic sultan.

This musician is playing a drum

This musician is playing a harp

The sultan being entertained

◄ This is an illustration for a copy of the *Maqamah* of al-Hariri. Al-Hariri wrote the *Maqamah* in the early twelfth century, and it became a popular text for copying and illustrating.

Surgical instruments are among the types of metal objects that have been recovered from archaeological sites

This illustration shows a scene in which a doctor 'bleeds' a patient; cutting the skin to allow the blood to flow out was thought to relieve many ailments

A curious crowd gathers around the scene

Literature

There was already a strong tradition of literature and storytelling in Arabic life before the time of Muhammad ﷺ. As the word of Islam spread, so did the Arabic language, and the literary tradition was maintained and continued. Poetry was used to express feelings about a wide variety of issues, from love to politics. Places such as Abbasid Baghdad became cultural centres where poets went to seek royal patronage (financial backing). From the tenth century onwards, the *maqamah* – the session or assembly – became popular. This was a form of prose writing that involved a series of dramatic episodes all featuring the same hero. Many copies were made of the *Maqamah* of al-Hariri.

Chess

Numerous images of people playing chess, as well as many carved chess pieces, have survived from the Islamic world. The origins of chess are uncertain, but it seems that the game was introduced into Persia from India some time during the sixth century. The earliest known chess piece dates from the early seventh century.

Pastimes

Music and poetry were two of the courtly pastimes in the Islamic world. Others included hunting, falconry, and watching sports such as wrestling. Evidence for all of these entertainments is found in miniature paintings and elsewhere. Polo was a sport that was introduced into the Islamic world by the Mongols, who found it to provide an excellent training for their nimble horses and their riders. There are paintings of Mongol games, while in Samarkand the polo grounds built for the fourteenth-century conqueror Timur can still be seen. In Isfahan the original stone goalposts used for polo during the time of the **Safavid** ruler Shah Abbas still stand.

◄ This chess piece shows a king enthroned on an elephant. It is carved from ivory, and was made in the eighth or ninth centuries by an Arab carver, who signed it.

Science and learning

Great emphasis was placed on learning and scholarship in Muslim society. For Muslims the core of all knowledge lay in the Qur'an, and studying the Qur'an and the life of the Prophet Muhammad ﷺ was an important act of worship. The great Islamic rulers all encouraged scholarship at their courts. The main areas of achievement were in astronomy, medicine and mathematics. Many Islamic cities had large libraries, and *madrasahs* (Islamic colleges) were built in towns and cities all over the Islamic world.

The importance of learning

Students were taught in a group by one of the *ulama* (teachers). They had to learn texts off by heart. When they could recite them perfectly, they were given a licence that listed the names of all the people who had taught the text, going back to the original author. This method of transmitting knowledge was based on the way in which the Prophet Muhammad ﷺ had passed on the messages he received from Allah.

In cities such as Baghdad and Cairo, large libraries housed thousands of books and manuscripts. Muslim scholars studied works from many sources including ancient Greece, Persia and India. The works of ancient Greek physicians such as Galen, who wrote about medicine, and Dioscorides, who described nearly 600 different plants in his botanical works, were studied, translated and illustrated. In the ninth century, the Abbasid ruler al-Mamun set up a 'House of Learning' in Baghdad especially for the study of the sciences. The numbers we use today (and call Arabic numerals) date from this time.

▼ This image from an Islamic manuscript shows three students sitting at the feet of their teacher, the ancient Greek statesman Solon.

Ibn Sina (980–1037)

Known in the West as Avicenna, Ibn Sina was a talented child who had memorized the Qur'an by the age of ten. By the time he was seventeen, he was a well-known physician. He wrote over 200 works on the sciences and philosophy, but his best-known work was the *al-Qanun fi at-Tibb* (*The Canon of Medicine*). In these books, Ibn Sina summarized the practices of ancient Greek physicians such as Galen and Hippocrates, as well as describing his own experiments. He also listed more than 700 drugs sold by Islamic pharmacists, commenting on their use and effectiveness. *The Canon of Medicine* was translated into Latin in the twelfth century, and became the standard work of reference in both the Islamic and Western worlds for centuries after.

▶ A page from the *al-Qanun fi at-tibb* (*The Canon of Medicine*) by Ibn Sina.

The astrolabe was used to show how the sky looked at a specific time and place

The astrolabe is made from copper

A 'map' of the sky is drawn on the face of the astrolabe

The rings were moved to set them to the correct positions

Astronomy and cartography

Many Muslim rulers and scholars took a keen interest in astronomy. Several famous observatories were built across the Islamic world, including one in Samarkand, founded by the fifteenth-century Timurid ruler Ulugh Beg, and one in Istanbul, constructed in 1580. Observations of the stars were made using devices such as the **armillary sphere** and the astrolabe. There were no telescopes before their invention in Europe in the seventeeth century. Instruments such as the astrolabe also helped with navigation. The land and sea trade networks that existed across and beyond the Islamic world encouraged the study of geography. One of the earliest maps of the known world was produced by an Arab called al-Idrisi (1100–66), who studied at Córdoba. Mapmaking flourished in the sixteenth century under the Ottomans, mainly as a result of the Ottoman conquests.

◀ This astrolabe was made in Iraq in the ninth century. Astrolabes were used to find the time during the day or night, work out the time of events such as sunrise or sunset, and to find the positions of stars.

35

Religion

From the earliest times, the mosque provided the focus for every Islamic community. The first mosques were probably modelled on the house of the Prophet Muhammad ﷺ in Madinah, which was used during his lifetime for prayer. The house was built around a square courtyard, with mud-brick walls. At the north and south ends the trunks of palm trees supported a flat roof, which gave some shelter from the sun. The design of seventh-century mosques at Basra and Kufa (both in Iraq) reflect this plan.

Women at prayer

The sixteenth-century Iranian manuscript on page 37 shows a ruler and his courtiers attending prayer in a mosque. The women, veiled for modesty, are in a separate area. Women were allowed to pray in mosques in many, but not all, Muslim societies. There were separate areas for men and women to enter a mosque, and for **wudu**, the ritual washing before prayer. However, women were generally encouraged to say their prayers at home.

Minarets

In the time of Muhammad ﷺ, the **adhan** (call to prayer) was given from the roof of the Prophet's house. The **minaret** came into use after the Prophet's death, and the first examples were probably built in Syria or Egypt. A man called a *muezzin* called all Muslims to prayer from the minaret. The Great Mosque at Samarra had a conical minaret, but the more usual shape was a tall, slender, often highly decorated tower. Most mosques had one minaret, but some had multiple minarets – particularly the lavish mosques built in Istanbul under the **Ottomans**. The Sulaimaniye Mosque has four minarets, while the mosque of Sultan Ahmed has six.

▼ This illustration is taken from an Iranian manuscript called *Majalis al-'Ushshaq* (*The Assemblies of the Lovers*). It dates from 1552.

The *minbar*

The Prophet Muhammad ﷺ delivered sermons to his followers from a simple pulpit – a high seat with three steps – situated in the shade of the southern side of the courtyard. From this came the **minbar**, the pulpit situated to the right of the *mihrab* that became a feature of most mosques. From here the imam, the leader of communal prayer, delivered his Friday sermon. In many cases, the *minbar* had three steps, like the one used by the Prophet ﷺ. But in many parts of the Islamic world, more elaborate versions came into use.

In the main area of the mosque, the men listen to a sermon

The women's area of the mosque

Small children sat with the women

▼ The *qiblah* wall in the Sultan Hasan mosque in Cairo, Egypt, built in the fourteenth century.

This is the mihrab, *which indicates the qiblah (direction of prayer)*

This is the minbar

The *mihrab*

In the early days at Madinah, the Prophet Muhammad ﷺ and his followers faced towards Jerusalem while praying. But in 624, Muhammad ﷺ received a message from Allah instructing him to pray in the direction of Makkah in Saudi Arabia. Accordingly, prayers were said facing towards the south wall of the house. This became the **qiblah** – the direction of Makkah to which Muslim prayer is always oriented. After Muhammad's death, the *qiblah* came to be indicated in mosques by a niche, called a **mihrab**. This became the focal point of the mosque, and was often highly decorated.

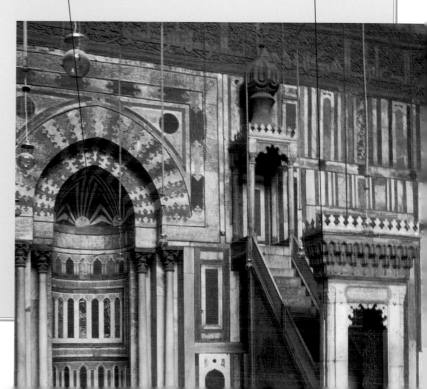

The Five Pillars

For Muslims, the teachings of Islam cover all aspects of life. These teachings include five special duties, often called the Five Pillars of Islam, which all Muslims must perform. They are: *shahadah*, bearing witness; *salah*, prayer; *zakah*, religious tax; *sawm*, fasting; and *hajj*, pilgrimage. Since the time of Muhammad ﷺ, these duties have shaped everyday life for Muslims all over the world. Their importance is reflected in many aspects of Islamic art.

The *Shahadah*

The words of the *Shahadah* are *There is no god but Allah and Muhammad is the Messenger of Allah*. The use of the words of the *Shahadah* as decorative **calligraphic** inscriptions was a constant reminder to Muslims of the importance of the message of Allah. The second half of the *Shahadah* reminded Muslims that Muhammad ﷺ was the messenger of Allah, and that it was the message itself (and not the messenger) that was most important. This emphasis was reflected in the avoidance of images in Islamic sacred art.

▶ This prayer rug comes from Turkestan in Central Asia. The design reflects the shape of a *mihrab*.

Friday mosques

Throughout the Islamic world, 'Friday mosques' were built that were big enough to hold the congregation for the special Friday service. The Arabic word *masjid* (mosque) means 'place of prostrations (bowing down)', and *salah* involves a particular ritual of movements and words that is performed on the floor. As a result, mosques have little furniture – instead Muslims often carry a small prayer carpet on which to carry out *salah*.

Salah and *zakah*

Muslims are required to pray five times a day, at set times. They do not attend the mosque for all of these prayers, but midday prayers on Fridays are compulsory for all Muslim men. *Zakah* is a religious tax by which all Muslims give between 2.5 and 10 per cent of their wealth or income to those who are less fortunate than themselves.

Sawm

During the month of Ramadan, Muslims observe a fast. For thirty days, they do not eat or drink during the hours of daylight. They recall the time that the Prophet Muhammad ﷺ received the first revelations from Allah. The end of this time of fasting is traditionally a time of celebration.

▶ This illustration is from the *Maqamah* of al-Hariri (see page 33). It shows celebrations at the end of Ramadan.

The flags bear religious inscriptions

Two men are blowing into long trumpets

Two kettle drums are mounted on a horse's back

This pilgrim is touching the black stone that is set into the side of the Ka'bah

The Ka'bah was later covered with a black cloth, called the kiswah

The pilgrims wear special clothes, each made from two pieces of white cloth

Hajj

The *hajj* is the pilgrimage to Makkah, which every Muslim must try to undertake once in his or her lifetime. The origin of the *hajj* is the pilgrimage made by the Prophet Muhammad ﷺ from Madinah to Makkah shortly before his death. In the early Islamic world, *hajj* caravans were organized from Cairo, Damascus and Baghdad.

These caravans were very profitable for the traders who organized them, and for the nomadic peoples of the Arabian desert, through which the caravans passed on their way to Makkah. Thousands of people travelled with these caravans, and it took great organization to supply them with water and food through the desert. Such a huge and regular movement of people from all corners of the Islamic world encouraged the interchange and mixing of ideas, as well as promoting trade.

◀ This fifteenth-century painting shows pilgrims around the **Ka'bah** in Makkah. Circling the Ka'bah is an important part of the *hajj*. The illustration comes from a book about religious observance.

The Qur'an

The **Qur'an** is the sacred book of all Muslims. It contains the revelations from Allah given to the Prophet Muhammad ﷺ by the Angel Jibril. The revelations were collected together in a written version after Muhammad's death to form the Qur'an. Muslims believe that the Qur'an is the word of Allah, and that not one single word was added or changed by Muhammad ﷺ.

The earliest Qur'ans

The Prophet Muhammad ﷺ learned each revelation off by heart as it was revealed to him (*Qur'an* means 'recitation' in Arabic). The revelations were later written down on a variety of materials – sheep bones, pieces of pottery, bits of leather. Muhammad ﷺ also taught the revelations to his followers, and they were recited during worship.

A person who knew the complete text of the Qur'an was known as a *hafiz* (plural: *huffaz*). After the death of the Prophet ﷺ, the first **Khalifah**, Abu Bakr ﷺ, assembled the *huffaz* and ordered a complete written version of the Qur'an to be made in one book. During the time of the third *Khalifah*, Uthman ﷺ, all other versions were checked against this text and any that differed were destroyed. Many copies were made of the standard text, and sent to cities all over the Islamic world. Today, just two survive – one in Tashkent in Uzbekistan, and one in Istanbul.

▼ This Qur'an dates from the ninth or tenth century. The words are written in **kufic** script (see page 42). The Qur'an is made from vellum.

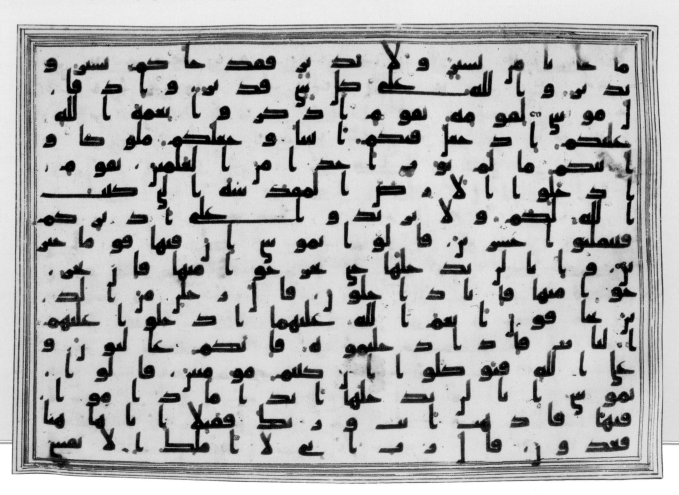

The impact of the Qur'an

The words of the Qur'an are at the heart of the Islamic faith. Copying the Qur'an was an act of worship practised by male and female Muslims down the centuries in all parts of the Islamic world. The letters on the page were themselves made as beautiful as possible in order to be worthy of the divine words being written – the art of **calligraphy**. The words of the Qur'an were frequently used to decorate the surfaces of buildings such as mosques, tombs and *madrasahs*, as well as mosque furniture such as lamps.

The art of the Qur'an

In keeping with Islamic tradition, the Qur'an was not illustrated with any images. However, beautiful, richly decorated Qur'ans were produced in all parts of the Islamic world. In Egypt, the Mamluks (former Turkish slaves who founded a dynasty in Egypt and Syria between 1250 and 1517) were renowned for the production of lavish and beautiful Qur'ans. In particular, three Qur'ans copied for Sultan Shaban II (reigned 1363–76) in *muhaqqaq* script are notable for the refined and detailed quality of the work.

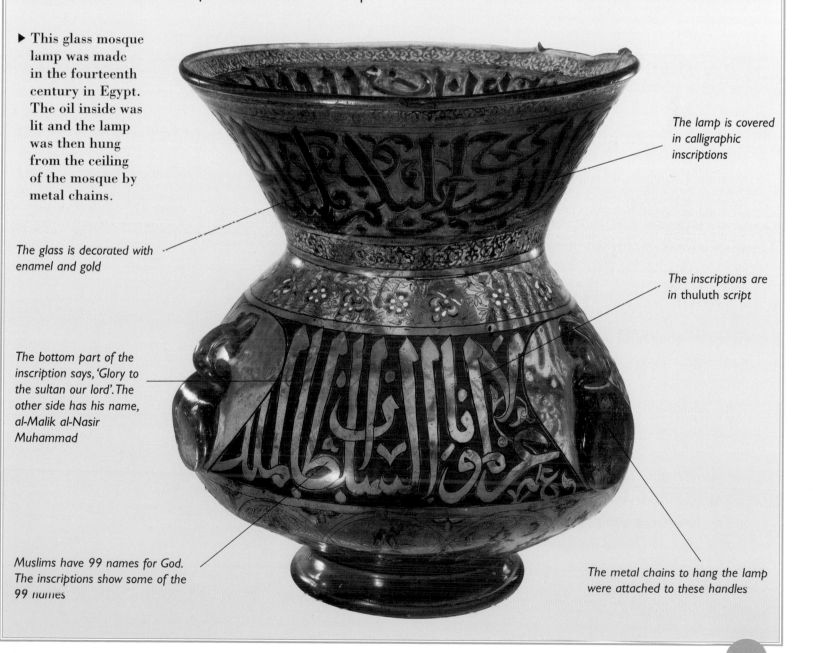

▶ This glass mosque lamp was made in the fourteenth century in Egypt. The oil inside was lit and the lamp was then hung from the ceiling of the mosque by metal chains.

The lamp is covered in calligraphic inscriptions

The glass is decorated with enamel and gold

The inscriptions are in thuluth *script*

The bottom part of the inscription says, 'Glory to the sultan our lord'. The other side has his name, al-Malik al-Nasir Muhammad

Muslims have 99 names for God. The inscriptions show some of the 99 names

The metal chains to hang the lamp were attached to these handles

Calligraphy

The highest of all the Islamic arts is calligraphy – the art of beautiful writing. The importance of calligraphy stemmed from the Muslim belief that the Qur'an is the literal word of Allah. Schools of calligraphy were established throughout the Islamic world, and both men and women became accomplished and famous scribes.

Styles of calligraphy

Arabic script is written and read from right to left. It is a Semitic script, in the same family as Hebrew and Ethiopic. Its origins lie in the script of the Nabateans – **nomads** who established a kingdom with its capital at Petra (in modern-day Jordan) in the late seventh and early sixth centuries BCE. As schools of calligraphy were established through the Islamic world, different styles of writing emerged. The two oldest styles were *kufic* – named after the town of Kufa, which was an early centre of calligraphy – and *naskhi*. *Kufic* was an angular script, well-suited to surface decoration in stone and mosaic. It was also used for early Qur'ans. *Naskhi* was a more flowing style, used also for secular writing.

As styles of calligraphy became more refined, they also became more varied. Different types of *kufic* and *naskhi* scripts were developed. For example, Eastern *kufic* was an elegant and refined angular script, while six flowing scripts became the classical scripts of Islamic calligraphy – *naskhi*, *thuluth*, *muhaqqaq*, *rayhani*, *riqa* and *tauqi*.

▲ This **Mughal** painting shows a scribe (right) and a painter at work.

Ibn al-Bawwab

Ibn al-Bawwab (d.1022) was one of the most famous calligraphers at the **Abbasid** court in Baghdad. He learned his art from the daughter of another famous calligrapher, Ibn Muqla, who worked at the Abbasid court at the beginning of the tenth century. Ibn Muqla was responsible for developing the classical scripts of Islamic calligraphy. Ibn al-Bawwab is said to have known the Qur'an off by heart, and to have copied it 64 times during his lifetime. However, only one copy is known to have survived.

▲ The inscriptions around the Dome of the Rock in Jerusalem are written in giant *kufic* script.

The headings are in the ornamental thuluth *script*

The main body of the text is in naskhi *script*

The script is read from right to left

◄ This Qur'an, copied by Ibn al-Bawwab, is the earliest surviving Qur'an to be written in *naskhi* script on paper. Earlier Qur'ans were usually written on vellum, a type of parchment made from animal skin.

Timeline

c.570

birth of Muhammad ﷺ

610

Muhammad ﷺ receives first messages from the Angel Jibril

622

the *hijrah* – migration to Madinah

632

death of Muhammad ﷺ; Abu Bakr ﷺ becomes **Khalifah**

634

death of Abu Bakr ﷺ; Umar ﷺ becomes *Khalifah*

634–44

Muslim armies invade Syria, Egypt and Iraq

638

Muslim armies capture Jerusalem

644

Umar ﷺ is assassinated and Uthman ﷺ becomes *Khalifah*

644–50

Muslim armies invade Iran and Afghanistan, and move into North Africa

656

Uthman ﷺ assassinated; Ali ﷺ becomes *Khalifah*.

661

Ali ﷺ assassinated; Mu'awiya I founds **Umayyad** dynasty

685

work starts on the Dome of the Rock in Jerusalem

705

work starts on the Great Mosque in Damascus

750

Abbasids seize power from Umayyads

756

Abd al-Rahman defeats Abbasid ruler and establishes al-Andalus in southern Spain

762–3

Baghdad founded as capital of Abbasid Empire

784

work starts on the Great Mosque of Córdoba

c.836

Abbasids move their capital from Baghdad to Samarra

892

Abbasid capital returns to Baghdad

969

Fatimids defeat Abbasids in Egypt

973

Fatimids establish capital at Cairo

990s

Seljuk Turks convert to Islam

ایں اسپ ارحہ ہو نہ حمہ او دیدہ... [Persian/Arabic inscription]

1055

Seljuk sultan Tughril-beg takes over Baghdad

1169

Salah ad-Din seizes power in Egypt

1171

Salah ad-Din proclaims return to **Sunni** Islam in Egypt

1206

Mongols form confederation of tribes under leader Genghis Khan

1258

Mongols sack Baghdad and bring Abbasid rule to an end

1380s–1405

Timur establishes control over much of Central Asia, Iran and Iraq

1453

Ottomans capture Constantinople and rename it Istanbul

1492

Granada, the last Muslim stronghold in Spain, is captured by the troops of the Catholic monarchs, Ferdinand and Isabella

1501

Safavids capture Tabriz and found their empire

1520–66

rule of Ottoman sultan Sulaiman 'the Magnificent'

1526–30

rule of first **Mughal** emperor, Babur

1556–1605

rule of Mughal emperor Akbar the Great

1588–1629

rule of Safavid Shah Abbas the Great

1597

work starts on new Safavid capital at Isfahan

1627–58

rule of Mughal emperor Shah Jahan

Glossary

Abbasids dynasty that held the title of *Khalifah* from 750 until 1258

adhan call to prayer

Almohad Berber people from North Africa who defeated the Almoravids for control of al-Andalus in 1147

Almoravid Berber people from the western Sahara who took control of al-Andalus in the eleventh century

armillary sphere large wooden astronomical instrument used to plot the orbits of stars and planets

bazaar covered market, usually containing many small shops

BCE 'before common era' – before the birth of Jesus Christ

Berber native inhabitant of North Africa

Byzantine from the empire of Byzantium, the eastern Roman Empire

calligraphy art of beautiful handwriting

caravanserai medieval inn on a trade route

CE after the death of Jesus Christ

Fatimids dynasty that ruled in North Africa and Egypt from 909 until 1171

harem women's quarters in a Muslim home

iwan vaulted, open-air hall

Ka'bah cube structure in Makkah towards which all Muslims direct their prayer

Khalifah (successor) title given to the successors of the Prophet Muhammad ﷺ

kufic type of angular Arabic script, named after the town of Kufa in Iraq

lustre type of glaze that contains a metallic pigment

madrasah Islamic college

mausoleum large and grand tomb

mihrab niche in the wall of a mosque that indicates the direction of prayer

minaret tower from which a muezzin issues the *adhan*

minbar pulpit in a mosque from where the address is given during Friday prayers

Mongols nomadic people from Central Asia who formed an empire in the thirteenth century

Mughals dynasty of Muslim emperors who ruled India from 1526 until 1857

naskhi type of Arabic script with a flowing style

Night of Ascent according to Muslim belief, the night when the Prophet Muhammad ﷺ ascended from a rock on the Temple Mount in Jerusalem into the heavens

nomad member of a people that roams from place to place to find fresh pasture for their animals

Ottomans dynasty of Turkish sultans who ruled Anatolia and much of the Mediterranean and the Middle East from the fourteenth century until 1922

pigment substance that gives something colour

qiblah the direction of prayer for all Muslims, which is towards Makkah

Qur'an the sacred book of Islam. Muslims believe that the Qur'an is the literal word of Allah, as given to the Prophet Muhammad ﷺ in the messages delivered by the Angel Jibril.

Rashidun the 'rightly guided ones', the first four *Khalifahs* after the death of the Prophet Muhammad: Abu Bakr (632–34), Umar (634–44), Uthman (644–56), Ali (656–61) [Peace Be Upon Them].

Safavids dynasty of Shi'a Muslims who ruled Iran from 1502 until 1736

Sasanians the rulers of Persia from 224 CE until their defeat by the Muslim armies in 651

Seljuks Turkish nomads from Central Asia who converted to Islam in the 990s and seized power from the Abbasids in the eleventh century

Shahadah Muslim declaration of faith: 'There is no god but Allah and Muhammad is the Messenger of Allah'

Shi'a Muslims Muslims who believe that leadership of the Islamic community passed directly to Ali ﷺ, as the closest blood relative of the Prophet Muhammad ﷺ, and through Ali's descendants

sunnah model practices, customs and traditions of the Prophet Muhammad ﷺ

Sunni Muslims who believe in the successorship of the first four *Khalifahs* – the *Rashidun*

Umayyads first Islamic dynasty, which ruled from 661 until 750

Uzbeks Turkish Mongol tribes who converted to Islam in the fourteenth century

wudu ritual washing before prayer

Further resources

Books

Bloom, Jonathan and Blair, Sheila, *Islamic Arts* (Phaidon, 1997)

Brend, Barbara, *Islamic Art* (The British Museum Press, 1991)

Insoll, Timothy, *The Archaeology of Islam* (Blackwells, 1999)

Morris, Neil, *The Atlas of Islam* (Barron's Educational, 2003)

Talbot Rice, David, *Islamic Art* (Thames and Hudson, 1975)

Wintle, Justin, *The Rough Guide: History of Islam* (Rough Guides, 2003)

Websites

www.metmuseum.org/toah/hd/orna/hd_orna.htm
The website of the Metropolitan Museum, New York, with links to many aspects and periods of Islamic art.

www.metmuseum.org/explore/Flowers/HTM/cata_fs.htm
Metropolitan Museum site about Mughal carpets.

www.lacma.org/islamic_art/intro.htm
The Los Angeles County Museum of Art site.

www.islamicart.com/
General site about Islamic art.

Index

Titles in the *History in Art* series include:

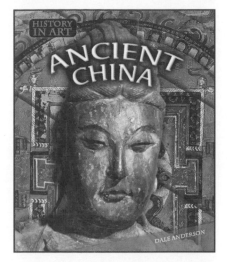

Hardback   1 844 43369 2

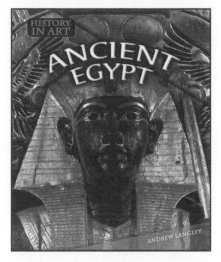

Hardback   1 844 43361 7

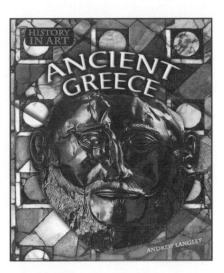

Hardback   1 844 43359 5

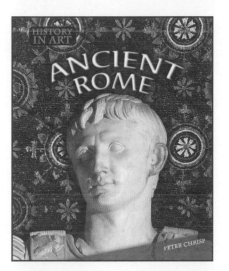

Hardback   1 844 43360 9

Hardback   1 844 43362 5

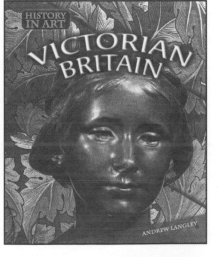

Hardback   1 844 43370 6

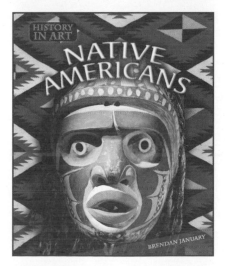

Hardback   1 844 43371 4

Hardback   1 844 43372 2

Hardback   1 844 43373 0

Find out about the other titles in this series on our website www.raintreepublishers.co.uk